THE UNITED STATES PRESIDENTS

ZACHARY
TAYLOR

OUR 12TH PRESIDENT

by Carol Brunelli

The Child's World®
childsworld.com

1980 Lookout Drive • Mankato, MN 56003-1705
800-599-READ • www.childsworld.com

ACKNOWLEDGMENTS

Content Adviser: David R. Smith, Adjunct Assistant
Professor of History, University of Michigan–Ann Arbor

PHOTOS

Cover and page 3: © Huntington Library, Art Museum,
and Botanical Gardens/Bridgeman Images (detail)
Interior: © Christie's Images/Bridgeman Images, 5; akg-images/
Newscom, 34; Bridgeman Images, 16, 28; Design Pics/
Newscom, 12; Everett Historical/Shutterstock.com, 14, 33, 38
(left), 39 (right); GRANGER, 13; Library of Congress, Prints and
Photographs Division, 4, 10, 19, 20, 21, 22, 23, 24, 25, 27, 36;
National Portrait Gallery, Smithsonian Institution; partial gift of
the Quaker Oats Company, 7; North Wind Picture Archives, 11,
26, 29, 30, 31, 32; Picture History/Newscom, 6, 9, 38 (right);
The History Collection/Alamy Stock Photo, 8; The Print Collector
Heritage Images/Newscom, 15, 39 (left); Universal Images
Group/Newscom, 37; World History Archive/Newscom, 18

ISBN 9781503844049 (REINFORCED LIBRARY BINDING)
ISBN 9781503847255 (PORTABLE DOCUMENT FORMAT)
ISBN 9781503848443 (ONLINE MULTI-USER EBOOK)
LCCN 2019957728

Printed in the United States of America

CONTENTS

This portrait of Zachary Taylor was painted in 1847.

CHAPTER ONE

OLD ROUGH
AND READY

On November 24, 1784, Zachary Taylor was born in his parents' native state of Virginia, but he was almost born in Kentucky. In the early fall, his parents, two brothers, and other settlers had set out from their home in Virginia for the wilds of Kentucky. The government had given Taylor's father a large piece of land in Kentucky as payment for serving in the Continental army during the American Revolution. The party stopped for a time at the country place of a friend, near the town of Barboursville in north-central Virginia. There, Sarah Strother Taylor, just twenty-three years old, gave birth to her third son, Zachary.

The Taylors eventually continued on to Beargrass Creek, near Louisville, Kentucky. They worked long days, carving their farm out of the thick forest. Taylor's earliest memories were of doing chores on his family's tobacco **plantation** with his seven brothers and sisters.

Like his father, Zachary Taylor served in the US military. Taylor's long, successful military career would take him all the way to the presidency.

Although Zachary Taylor was born in Virginia, he grew up on his family's tobacco plantation in Kentucky, a part of America's frontier. It was hard work to farm the forested area, and settlers often had to fight Native Americans to keep control of their land.

Their plantation did well, as did those of their neighbors. But such success came with a price. The settlers were in Native American **territory,** and the Native Americans fought to keep control of their land. Skirmishes between Native Americans and white settlers were common. From an early age, Zachary Taylor learned that America's new **frontier** was both a place of great opportunity and of great danger.

Taylor's father, Richard, had been a lieutenant colonel during the American Revolution. He served with General George Washington. Taylor's cousin, James Madison, was the fourth president of the United States. Another cousin, Robert E. Lee, later led **Confederate** troops during the **Civil War.**

When Taylor was born, the United States was only eight years old. The US Constitution had not yet been written, and there were only 13 states.

In 1808, James Madison, then the US **secretary of state,** recommended Taylor for military service. The 23-year-old Taylor began a long, **distinguished** military career that would take him all the way to Washington, DC. He first entered the army as a lieutenant in the **infantry.** Two years later, on June 21, 1810, he married Margaret "Peggy" Mackall Smith. Their marriage lasted more than 40 years. Taylor would spend nearly all of those years as a military officer.

The Taylors had five daughters and one son. Two of the girls died in infancy. Two of the surviving girls married military officers. Taylor's youngest daughter, Betty, would play an important role in her father's life.

Margaret Taylor did not like fancy parties. She refused to serve as White House hostess while her husband was president.

William Bliss (standing) was charming and talented. He could speak 13 languages.

When he was elected president, she became his first lady, or hostess at the White House. Betty and her husband, William Bliss, were close to Taylor. Bliss was Taylor's trusted friend and adviser, serving as his private secretary during the Mexican-American War and during his presidency. Taylor referred to him as "Perfect Bliss," a nickname Bliss had earned as a student, because of his good grades and neat appearance.

Taylor was taught at home and had only a basic education. All his life, he was considered a poor speller.

During his many battles, Taylor often wore baggy cotton pants, a long coat, and a wide-brimmed straw hat instead of a uniform. His appearance and tough character earned Taylor the nickname "Old Rough and Ready."

Taylor's oldest child, Sarah Knox, was named after Fort Knox, the fort where her father was stationed when she was born. When "Knox" was a teenager, the Taylors moved to Fort Crawford. It was here that she met her future husband, Jefferson Davis, the man who would become the president of the Confederate States of America. Taylor opposed their marriage because he knew firsthand the hardships of military life. "I will be damned if another daughter of mine shall marry into the Army," he once wrote. "I know enough of the family life of officers. I scarcely know my own children or they me." Taylor also pointed out, "I have no personal objections to Lieutenant Davis." When Sarah Taylor and Jefferson Davis married a few years later, Zachary Taylor and his wife did not attend their wedding.

As a soldier in the US Army, Taylor's main responsibility was protecting the frontier, which was expanding quickly to the west. He defended the **Union** against foreign nations, such as Great Britain and Mexico. He also fought Native Americans.

Sarah Taylor married Jefferson Davis in 1835. She died just three months later.

Zachary Taylor (pictured, with raised sword) led the US troops defending Fort Harrison during the War of 1812. The fort was in Indiana Territory, near what is now Terre Haute.

Taylor fought in the War of 1812 between the United States and Great Britain. The war had erupted because the British had been stopping American ships and forcing American sailors to join the British navy. When the war began, British troops and their Native American **allies** marched south from what is now Canada and captured one American fort after another. On September 4, 450 Native Americans, led by a Shawnee chief named Tecumseh, surrounded Fort Harrison on the Wabash River in Indiana and lit one of the buildings on fire. Taylor quickly ordered that the burning roof be torn off to save the rest of the buildings. Taylor and his men put the fire out and then fought Tecumseh's men. Indiana's governor praised Captain Taylor's "brave defense" of Fort Harrison, and the US Army rewarded him with a **promotion** to the rank of major.

Taylor spent the next few years in retirement from the army. Soon, the nation would call on this soldier once again to keep peace on the frontier. He spent much of the next 20 years in the present-day states of Iowa, Wisconsin, Minnesota, and Louisiana, training soldiers to defend forts along the Mississippi River.

In 1832, the army assigned Taylor, who was by then a colonel, to lead US soldiers once again. He took command of troops who were fighting Native Americans in the northwest corner of Illinois.

More and more white settlers in the region were moving onto Native American land. They were forcing the Sauk and the Fox people across the Mississippi River into Iowa. Led by Black Hawk, a Sauk leader, the Native Americans fought to get back their land. Taylor's men did not want to follow the Native Americans onto unsettled lands, but he pushed them across Illinois and into the Wisconsin wilderness. After the brutal Battle of Bad Axe, Black Hawk and his men surrendered.

Sauk and Fox people flee to new land in Wisconsin during the Battle of Bad Axe. Colonel Zachary Taylor and his soldiers defeated Black Hawk and his men in 1832.

In the state of Florida, the Seminole people were also resisting white settlement on their land. This led to the Second Seminole War, which lasted from 1835 until 1842. It was during this war that Taylor was given the nickname "Old Rough and Ready." He seemed to be unbeatable as he chased Seminoles through knee-deep mud and mosquito-infested swamps. The victory of Taylor's troops at the Battle of Okeechobee in 1837 earned him a promotion to general. He took command of all US troops in Florida. Taylor gained great fame in this war for his rough-and-ready fighting. He still was not well known to most Americans, though. The next war Taylor fought—the Mexican-American War—would change that. He didn't know it at the time, but Taylor was on his way to the presidency.

TAYLOR AND THE SEMINOLE NATION

The US Army often used violence to evict Native Americans from land that the US government wanted to claim. Sometimes, the army used dogs. In Florida, Taylor assured the government that dogs would be used only to locate the Native Americans. Instead, his soldiers allowed the animals to viciously attack Seminoles. Although American settlers wanted more land, not everybody approved of the government's way of getting it.

Still, Taylor was known to be a fair man. He tried to honor treaties made with the Native Americans and sometimes prevented white settlers from spreading onto Native American lands. In fact, when Taylor's troops captured African Americans who had escaped slavery and were fighting with the Seminole people, Taylor angered Southerners by refusing to return them to their owners. In the painting below, Taylor (on horseback) is leading US forces in battle against the Seminoles.

CHAPTER TWO

A NATIONAL HERO

Between 1840 and 1845, General Zachary Taylor retired from the frontier wars. He spent most of his time running his farms. Men who knew him spoke of his kind heart and gentleness. One man said, "I knew the old man well. He was kind, generous, but a little close with his money."

What he meant was that Taylor spent money carefully. Taylor's plan was to retire from the army with enough money that he would not have to depend on the government or anyone else to support him and his family.

But then President James K. Polk called General Taylor back into service. A war was brewing between Mexico and the United States. Taylor was to report to Texas immediately.

Taylor became famous for his success in the Mexican-American War. Many Americans admired that he fought side by side with his troops.

In 1836, Texas had won its independence from Mexico. After the war, Mexico and Texas disagreed on their border. Mexico insisted the border was the Nueces River. Texas claimed that it was the Rio Grande. Even before Texas was admitted to the Union on December 29, 1845, the United States and Mexico clashed in the disputed region.

General Taylor (on white horse) gives orders during the Battle of Buena Vista. In the battle, Taylor's 5,000 troops defeated 15,000 Mexican troops.

Taylor left his quiet life on the plantation and headed for Corpus Christi, Texas. From there, he marched his troops all the way to the banks of the Rio Grande. Taylor's troops arrived on March 28, 1846. They found a large Mexican army waiting for them just across the river. The armies waited and watched one another for weeks. Meanwhile, more troops arrived. Finally, on April 24, 1846, hundreds of Mexican soldiers crossed the river. They surrounded a group of American soldiers. All the Americans were killed or captured. When word of this reached General Taylor, he quickly informed President Polk that the war with Mexico had begun. The United States officially declared war on May 13.

In battle after battle, the American troops were outnumbered. Still, under the leadership of General Taylor, they never gave up or gave in. They won two big victories north of the Rio Grande in Texas and another in northern Mexico. Finally, Taylor marched his troops to a mountain pass near a ranch called Buena Vista. General Antonio López de Santa Anna and 15,000 Mexican soldiers headed his way. Taylor had just 5,000 men. He could have surrendered. After all, the odds were against a victory. But he refused to give up.

By all reports, it was his bravery that kept the troops in place under heavy fire and terrible odds. One officer raced up to the general and begged him to retreat. Taylor told him, "No, we will decide the battle here! I will never, alive, leave my wounded behind!"

He moved fearlessly from one position to another on his horse, Old Whitey. He demanded bravery from his men.

The appearance of the general on the front line gave his soldiers courage. Two shots sliced through Taylor's coat, but he barely noticed. He continued to shout orders and watch the fighting. After two days of fierce struggle, Santa Anna surrendered. Taylor had another unexpected victory.

In addition to his military career, Taylor was interested in farming. In 1823, he purchased a 380-acre (154-hectare) cotton plantation in Louisiana. Years later, he bought Cypress Grove, a much larger cotton plantation in Mississippi.

ANTONIO LÓPEZ DE SANTA ANNA: PRESIDENT AND GENERAL

Antonio López de Santa Anna (1794–1876) was at the center of Mexican **politics** and government for 40 years. As a young man, he fought against Mexican independence from Spain. Later, he became Mexico's chief general and president. He served as president of Mexico 11 times over a 22-year period.

In 1836, Santa Anna made history in Texas, leading the forces that overwhelmed the Alamo. The Texans remember him as being a particularly ruthless fighter. Despite this, he was allowed to return to Mexico after Texans captured him in the Battle of San Jacinto. He returned to battle in 1847 to lead Mexico's army of the north against the American forces led by General Zachary Taylor. At the time, he was also president of Mexico. By the end of that year, Mexico had surrendered to the United States. Soon after, Santa Anna stepped down from both the presidency and the army.

Like Zachary Taylor, General Winfield Scott (pictured) was an army commander and a hero of the Mexican-American War. He was nicknamed "Old Fuss and Feathers" because of his tidy uniform and love of ceremony.

Zachary Taylor's letters from the battlefield show little joy over the victory. He was surrounded by death and destruction, and this weighed heavily on him. In a letter to his brother Joseph, he wrote, "The great loss of life on both sides . . . has deprived me of everything like pleasure." He was certain, too, that there would have been fewer American **casualties** if he had not lost troops to another **expedition** led by General Winfield Scott. In a letter to Dr. Robert C. Wood, an army surgeon and husband of his eldest daughter, Ann, he wrote, "If Scott had left me five hundred or one thousand regular Infantry, the Mexican army would have been completely broken down."

In the United States, Americans were celebrating Taylor's victory at Buena Vista. He was a national hero. Some people believed the courageous man should run the country. Posters of "Old Rough and Ready" could be seen everywhere. Newspapers published stories about his military career and strong character. "Rough and Ready" clubs organized parades and **rallies** in support of a Taylor presidency. His popularity did not go unnoticed. It attracted the attention of the three major **political parties** of the day. Finally, Taylor decided to run with the **Whig Party.**

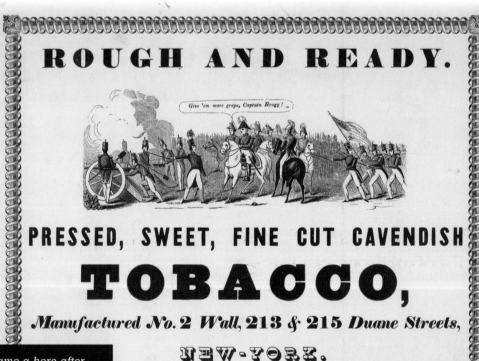

Taylor became a hero after his success in the Mexican-American War. His name and image appeared in advertisements and on posters. This tobacco label depicts Taylor on a battlefield.

Taylor was a slave owner from the South, so the Whig Party wanted a vice presidential candidate who would please antislavery Whigs in the North. They chose Millard Fillmore from New York.

Z. TAYLOR.

M. FILLMORE.

THE PEOPLE'S CHOICE FOR

PRESIDENT & VICE PRESIDENT

FROM 1849 TO 1853.

Presidential elections were just around the corner. Taylor had an excellent chance of winning. He was both famous and a man Americans could admire. Old Rough and Ready was a national hero, but he looked like a normal, hardworking American farmer.

The Whig Party knew that Taylor would probably win on his popularity alone. They also knew his military record would win him votes with Northerners, while the fact that he owned slaves would make Southerners comfortable with him. Taylor didn't discuss his opinions about **controversial** topics—especially whether to allow slavery in new states and territories. This kept him from making political enemies.

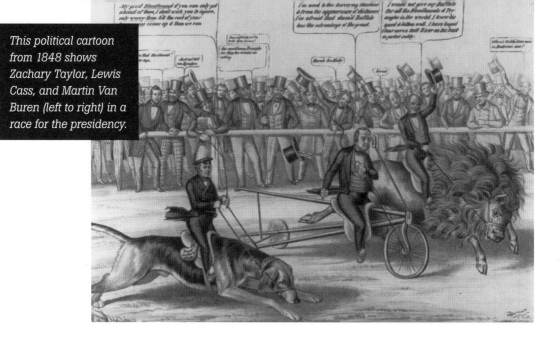

This political cartoon from 1848 shows Zachary Taylor, Lewis Cass, and Martin Van Buren (left to right) in a race for the presidency.

The Whig Party chose Millard Fillmore to run as the vice presidential **candidate.** Taylor's opponents were Lewis Cass of the Democratic Party and Martin Van Buren of the Free Soil Party. The main issue of the **campaign** was the Wilmot Proviso, which was a **bill** to ban slavery from any territory won in the Mexican-American War. Cass was against the Wilmot Proviso, and Van Buren was for it. Taylor would not say where he stood on the issue. In the end, Taylor won the election, and the Wilmot Proviso never passed.

Zachary Taylor was sworn in on March 5, 1849, as the 12th president of the United States. An estimated 10,000 people attended his **inauguration.** At the appearance of the old general, cheers of "rough and ready" followed. The cheers were magnified by the shooting of cannons. Taylor took the oath of office and then gave his inaugural speech. Pulling down eyeglasses that had been on his head, he delivered a speech that was simple, direct, and full of gratitude. Taylor thanked the American people for voting him into office even though he did not have experience in politics.

At the time, no one really knew what his political views were, especially on the slavery issue. After all, he tried not to discuss difficult topics during his campaign. But Americans would find out what he thought soon enough. This time, he would state his opinion for all to hear.

Taylor did not meet his vice president, Millard Fillmore, until after they won the election.

The election of November 7, 1848, was the first time a presidential election was held on the same day in every state.

Zachary Taylor was sworn in as president on March 5, 1849.

ABRAHAM LINCOLN SUPPORTS TAYLOR

During the presidential campaign of 1848, future president Abraham Lincoln took part in the **nomination** and election of General Zachary Taylor. Lincoln made speeches in Maryland and Massachusetts, as well as in his home state of Illinois. He encouraged young men to become active in American politics by forming "Rough and Ready" clubs, groups that held meetings and made speeches in favor of a Zachary Taylor presidency. His support helped Taylor win the election. During the campaign, Lincoln wrote:

Now as to the young men, you must not wait to be brought forward by the older men. For instance, do you suppose that I should ever have got into notice if I had waited to be hunted up and pushed forward by older men? You young men get together and form a "Rough and Ready" club, and have regular meetings and speeches. . . . Let every one play the part he can play best— some speak, some sing, and all "holler." Your meetings will be of evenings; the older men, and the women, will go to hear you; so that it will not only contribute to the election of "Old Zach," but will be an interesting pastime, and improving to the intellectual faculties of all engaged.

CHAPTER THREE

TOWARD ENDING SLAVERY

The 1848 Treaty of Guadalupe Hidalgo ended the Mexican-American War. It also added new territories to the Union. These territories would eventually become states, but would they be **free states** or slave states? That was the question the American people and Congress had to answer. Up to this point, the United States had an equal number of slave states and free states. Now Congress was setting the conditions for statehood in the western territories. The Missouri **Compromise** set the North–South border that divided the country into slave and free states. Not surprisingly, the South wanted this border to stretch all the way to the Pacific. Most Northerners wanted slavery banned in all new territories. Fiery **debates** erupted over this issue, threatening the Union. But who was better prepared to defend the Union than President Zachary Taylor, a national hero?

Zachary Taylor was the last candidate from the Whig Party to be elected president.

Under the Treaty of Guadalupe Hidalgo, the United States gained much of northern Mexico. Today, this area includes all of the states of California, Nevada, and Utah, along with parts of Arizona, Colorado, New Mexico, and Wyoming.

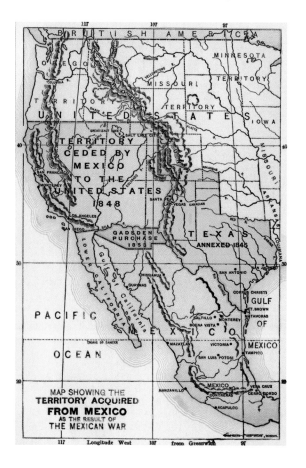

Taylor was a cotton planter and slave owner. He did not want to end slavery, but he was against extending it into new states such as California, Utah, and New Mexico. His position angered Southerners. He was a Southerner, he owned two plantations, and he enslaved more than 100 African Americans. How could he oppose slavery? How could he support the North?

In fact, Taylor did not support the North. He respected slaveholders' rights in the states where slavery was legal. But the spread of slavery was controversial. He thought it might tear the country apart, so he did not support it. To Taylor, it was more important to **preserve** the Union than to extend slavery.

After the Mexican-American War, the United States gained about 1.2 million square miles (3.1 million sq km) of new territory. This land is shown in pink on the map.

He made his point clear when he said, "We must . . . preserve the Union at all hazards. Upon its preservation must depend our own happiness and that of countless **generations** to come. Whatever dangers may threaten it, I stand by it."

Taylor's army horse, Old Whitey, often grazed on the White House lawn. Visitors to the White House sometimes took souvenir hairs from Old Whitey.

ATTACK ON CUBA

The war with Mexico greatly increased the territory of the United States and made some Americans hungry for more land. Spain controlled Cuba at the time. Some Cubans in the United States and Southerners who wanted to expand slavery started a movement to take over the island. Slavery was still legal in Cuba. The goal of the movement was to invade Cuba and make it part of the United States.

HO, FOR CUBA.

LIBERTY FOR ALL.

GRAND MASSMEETING

HUZZAH FOR LOPEZ.

The citizens of Washington and vicinity, are respectfully invited to attend a MASS MEETING, to be held in front of the PATENT OF- FICE, on Monday evening, Sept. 1. 1851 The object of the Meeting is to sympathise with the Patriots, and the friends of those who fell in their efforts to free Cuba from the tyran- ny of Spain.

Good speaking may be expected.

Narciso Lopez, a former Cuban governor, led the movement. The poster opposite announces a meeting in support of Lopez. President Taylor heard about the group's plans. He warned them that if they moved ahead, they would be punished.

The group ignored the president's threat. Lopez set sail for Cuba from Mexico. The Spanish captured 52 of his men before he even reached Cuba. When Lopez and his remaining men finally arrived in Cuba, they found themselves heavily outnumbered by Spanish troops. They turned around immediately, but the Spanish followed them. In the end, 70 Americans were killed.

True to his word, Taylor ordered the arrest of Lopez and his men. Taylor decided to help the 52 men who had been captured, however. They had not committed a crime, though they had planned to. He made an agreement with the Spanish for their release. In exchange, he promised that the United States would help the Spanish keep control of Cuba. The men were soon freed. The picture above shows Havana, Cuba, in the 19th century.

Arguments over slavery frequently boiled over in Taylor's time. In 1851, two congressmen from Mississippi got into a fistfight at the Capitol over how their state should deal with slavery.

When California and New Mexico became US territory, President Taylor encouraged them to quickly write their constitutions and apply to become states. By moving swiftly, he hoped to avoid the debate over slavery, but he did not succeed. Southerners were angry because they knew California and New Mexico opposed slavery. Members of Congress were angry because they thought the president was trying to take away their right to make laws.

Taylor owned 118 slaves at the time he was elected president. He bought 64 more along with a sugar plantation just weeks before he died.

Heated debates erupted in Congress over the slavery issue. Some congressmen even carried weapons, while others were involved in fistfights.

In the meantime, Senators John C. Calhoun of South Carolina, Daniel Webster of Massachusetts, and Henry Clay of Kentucky were discussing ideas that would keep the North and South at peace. Henry Clay believed that attacks on slavery must end and that slaveholders must have equal rights in the West. Clay believed that if these couldn't be accomplished, the North and the South should separate peacefully. In March 1850, Henry Clay introduced a set of proposals to Congress to prevent this from happening. These recommendations became known as the Compromise of 1850. The proposals gave both the North and the South part of what they wanted. For example, California could join the Union as a free state. This would please the North. The Fugitive Slave Act was included to please the South. This act said the government had to make sure all runaway slaves were returned to their owners. Before this act, runaway slaves were free if they reached the North.

Congressmen from the South threatened that if Taylor didn't change his views on the spread of slavery, Southern states would leave the Union. The president was furious. He said that if they dared rebel against the United States, he would "hang them with less reluctance than I had hung deserters and spies in Mexico!"

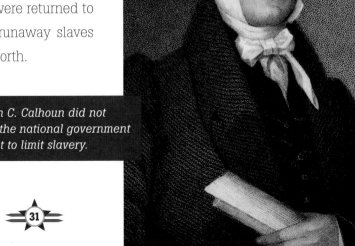

Senator John C. Calhoun did not believe that the national government had the right to limit slavery.

The Fugitive Slave Act required that police and other officials in the North arrest anyone suspected of being a runaway slave. In this picture, runaway slaves are captured in Boston, Massachusetts.

In 1849, President Zachary Taylor spoke at the funeral of Dolley Madison, the wife of former president James Madison. According to legend, Taylor referred to Mrs. Madison as the "First Lady." This may have been the first time this title was connected with a president's wife. No record of this speech exists today.

Taylor felt the compromise would allow the spread of slavery. He did not support any part of it that would favor the South. He wanted each proposal to be voted on separately. He hoped that some parts of it would pass and others would not. The proposals were debated in Congress, and some changes were made. The debate lasted until the final days of Taylor's presidency.

CHAPTER FOUR

FINAL DAYS OF A PRESIDENCY

The biggest issue in Zachary Taylor's presidency was the spread of slavery into new territories. This issue was not **resolved** during his brief 500 days as president. But Taylor did have his accomplishments. The territory of the United States had greatly increased. As a result, the Department of the Interior was created. The new department would take charge of managing public lands, natural **resources,** and Native American affairs. Perhaps Taylor's most important achievement concerned international affairs. Taylor and his assistants made sure that the United States would be able to use any Central American **canals** built in the future.

For some time, the United States had been planning to build a canal across Central America. Without a canal, ships had to sail around the southern tip of South America to travel from the Atlantic Ocean to the Pacific Ocean. In 1849, it appeared that Britain would take control of Central America. If this happened, any canal built there would be under British control. The British could refuse US ships access to the canal or charge high fees for its use.

Although Taylor's time as president was brief, he succeeded in increasing US territory and keeping the Union intact.

A tugboat passes through the Panama Canal on a test run in 1913. The canal officially opened in 1914.

In 1850, the Clayton-Bulwer Treaty between the United States and Great Britain guaranteed that any future canal constructed across Central America would be neutral. This meant that all nations would have fair and equal use of the canal. Decades later, the United States built a canal across Panama. Taylor's work on the Clayton-Bulwer Treaty had secured this important transportation route for future generations.

Zachary Taylor did not live to see the construction of a canal or resolve the debate over slavery. But he did hold together a nation that was growing and changing rapidly. If Taylor had been asked what his most important accomplishment was, he might have said it was the preservation of the Union. He once said, "For more than half a century, during which kingdoms and empires have fallen, this Union has stood unshaken. The patriots who formed it have long since descended to the grave; yet still it remains, the proudest monument to their memory."

During Taylor's time, the Union stood unshaken, but it would be torn apart 11 years later when the Civil War, the war between the North and South, began.

Taylor did not live long enough to fight this war. On the Fourth of July, 1850, there was a grand celebration in the capital at the Washington Monument. Taylor rode in a carriage to the monument grounds. It was a hot, humid day. The heat affected Taylor so much that he complained of dizziness and a headache when he got out of the carriage.

Taylor returned to the White House hot and exhausted. Trying to regain his strength, he ate a bowl of cherries and drank some iced milk. That evening, he had terrible stomach cramps. For the next five days, Taylor became weaker. Crowds of people waited outside the White House for news of the president's condition.

Taylor was a distant cousin of the 32nd president of the United States, Franklin D. Roosevelt.

President Taylor died just 16 months after taking office. Thousands of Americans came to watch his funeral procession (pictured) in July 1850.

Early in the day on July 9, a rumor spread that the president was dead. The White House quickly denied the report, saying the president was actually feeling better. The crowd outside cheered, and people ran to churches where they rang the bells to spread the good news. But by evening, the president's condition had worsened. He died at 10:30 p.m. His doctors believed that either the milk or the cherries contained deadly germs. The following day, Vice President Millard Fillmore took office as the 13th president of the United States.

Taylor was the second president to die from illness while in office. William Henry Harrison, the ninth president, died just one month after his inauguration.

Taylor's funeral was held on July 13. Thousands of Americans lined the route of the funeral **procession.** Taylor's trusted horse, Old Whitey, followed behind the carriage that held the president's body.

Soon after Taylor's death, Congress passed the Compromise of 1850 with President Fillmore's support. But the debate over slavery was far from over, as the Civil War would prove. Taylor's only son, Richard, served as a general in the Confederate army, the army that opposed the Union his father had fought so hard to protect.

POISON OR POOR HEALTH?

For many years, some people suspected that Zachary Taylor's death was not an accident. They believed he might have been murdered with a poison called arsenic. In 1991, Taylor's descendants wanted the question settled. Modern science can determine long after death if a person took poison. So in 1991, Taylor's remains were removed from the Zachary Taylor Memorial Cemetery in Louisville, Kentucky.

Samples of hair and fingernails were taken and tested in a laboratory. Scientists concluded that Taylor had indeed died of a severe stomach illness. This finding proved that Taylor's enemies were not guilty of murder.

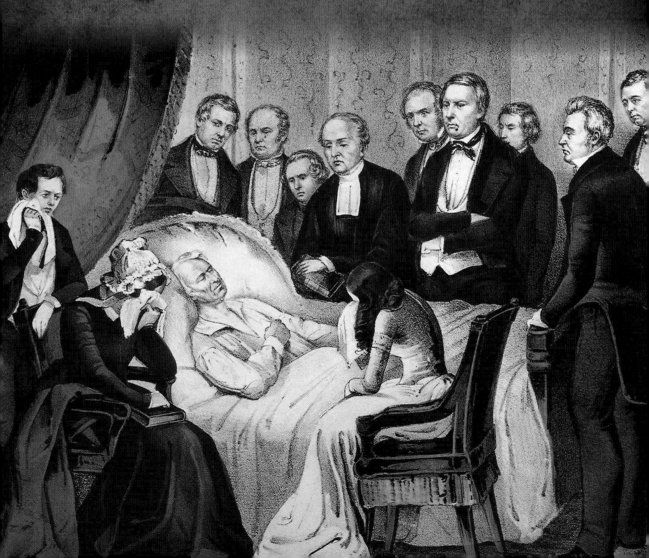

784
chary Taylor is born
ar the town of
rboursville, Virginia,
November 24.

785
e Taylor family
ttles in Beargrass
eek, near Louisville,
ntucky.

1790s
Taylor is taught reading, writing, and arithmetic at home. He works on his family's tobacco plantation. In his spare time, he enjoys hunting, fishing, and riding horseback through the woods.

1808
On May 3, Taylor enters the US Army as a first lieutenant in the infantry.

1810
On June 21, Taylor marries Margaret "Peggy" Mackall Smith. They will eventually have five daughters and a son.

1811
Taylor is promoted to the rank of captain and put in command of Fort Knox in Indiana Territory.

1812
The United States declares war on Great Britain, starting the War of 1812. Taylor takes command of Fort Harrison in Indiana Territory. On September 4, he defeats Native American forces led by Shawnee chief Tecumseh. Taylor is promoted to the rank of major.

1816–1818
Taylor is sent to Fort Howard in present-day Green Bay, Wisconsin, to protect fur trappers in the area who are battling Native Americans.

1819
Taylor is promoted to the rank of lieutenant colonel and is assigned to the southwest frontier of Louisiana.

1820	1830	1840		1850

1824
Taylor buys a cotton plantation north of Baton Rouge.

1828
Taylor trains soldiers to defend various forts along the Mississippi River.

1832
Taylor is promoted to full colonel and fights Black Hawk and his forces.

1835
The Second Seminole War begins. Taylor earns the nickname "Old Rough and Ready" during the war.

1838
Taylor fights his final battle against the Seminole people at Lake Okeechobee and is promoted to rank of brigadier general.

1841
Taylor is put in charge of an area covering parts of the Louisiana, Arkansas, and Oklahoma territories. He oversees construction of forts and inspects border forts. In December, he buys a large plantation, Cypress Grove, in Jefferson County, Mississippi. By then, he owns more than 100 enslaved African Americans.

1845
President James K. Polk sends Taylor to Texas to prepare for an invasion by Mexican forces. On December 29, Texas becomes the 28th state to join the Union.

1846
Mexican forces attack US forces in Texas on April 24. Taylor's men win the battles of Palo Alto and Resaca de la Palma. The Mexican-American War officially begins on May 13. Taylor is promoted to major general.

1847
The Battle of Buena Vista begins on February 22. Taylor leads troops to victory and becomes a national hero.

1848
The Treaty of Guadalupe Hidalgo is signed on February 2, ending the war with Mexico. The Whig political party nominates Taylor as its presidential candidate. On November 7, Taylor is elected president of the United States.

1849
Taylor resigns from the US Army in January. On March 5, he is sworn in as the 12th president of the United States. The Department of the Interior is established. The California gold rush begins. Thousands of easterners go west to seek gold.

1850
Debates over the extension of slavery rage in Congress. Senator Henry Clay introduces proposals that will become known as the Compromise of 1850. In April, the United States and Great Britain agree on the Clayton-Bulwer Treaty, which states that any canal built across Central America can be used by all nations. On July 4, Taylor becomes ill with stomach cramps. He dies on July 9. Vice President Millard Fillmore is sworn in as the 13th president on July 10.

GLOSSARY

allies (AL-lize): Allies are nations that have agreed to help each other by fighting together against a common enemy. During the War of 1812, the Shawnee nation was a British ally, fighting against the United States.

bill (BILL): A bill is a proposed law presented to a group of lawmakers. Congress decides if a bill will become law.

campaign (kam-PAYN): A campaign is the process of running for an election, including activities such as giving speeches or attending rallies. Abraham Lincoln supported Whig candidate Zachary Taylor during his 1848 campaign.

canals (kuh-NALZ): Canals are human made waterways. The Clayton-Bulwer Treaty ensured that any canals built across Central America could be used by all nations.

candidate (KAN-duh-dayt): A candidate is a person running in an election. Several candidates run for president every four years.

casualties (KA-zhul-teez): In a war, casualties refer to the people who die, are injured, are missing, or are taken prisoner. There were tens of thousands of casualties in the Mexican-American War.

civil war (SIV-il WAR): A civil war is a war between opposing groups of citizens within the same country. The American Civil War began after the South left the Union.

compromise (KOM-pruh-myz): A compromise is a way to settle a disagreement in which both sides give up part of what they want. The US Senate created the Compromise of 1850 in an attempt to satisfy both the North and the South.

Confederate (kun-FED-ur-ut): Confederate refers to the slave states that left the Union in 1861. The people of these states were also called Confederates.

constitution (kon-stih-TOO-shun): A constitution is a document explaining the set of basic principles that governs a state, country, or society. California's constitution outlawed slavery.

controversial (kon-truh-VUR-shul): If something is controversial, people disagree and argue about it. A controversial topic in the election of 1848 was the expansion of slavery into the land acquired by the United States after the Mexican-American War.

debates (dih-BAYTZ): Debates are arguments about a certain subject. In 1850, there were heated debates in Congress about Henry Clay's compromise proposals.

descendants (dih-SEN-duntz): Descendants are people born after someone else within the same family, such as children and grandchildren. Some of Taylor's descendants believed he might have been poisoned.

distinguished (dih-STING-gwisht): If someone is distinguished, he or she is well known for positive accomplishments or deeds. Zachary Taylor was a distinguished military leader in the US Army.

expedition (ek-spuh-DIH-shun): In military terms, an expedition is another word for a campaign designed to achieve a specific goal. During the Mexican-American War, Taylor led an expedition in northern Mexico.

free states (FREE STAYTS): Free states are states that banned slavery in the period before the Civil War. Southerners did not want the nation to have more free states than slave states.

frontier (frun-TEER): A frontier is a region that is at the edge of or beyond settled land. During Zachary Taylor's lifetime, the American frontier was rapidly expanding into the west.

generations (jeh-nuh-RAY-shunz): Generations are groups of people born at the same time. Taylor wanted to preserve the Union for future generations.

inauguration (ih-naw-gyuh-RAY-shun): An inauguration is the ceremony that takes place when a new president begins a term. Taylor died just 16 months after his inauguration.

infantry (IN-fun-tree): An infantry is a group of soldiers trained to fight on foot. Zachary Taylor first entered the army in the infantry.

nomination (nah-mih-NAY-shun): If someone receives a nomination, he or she is chosen by a political party to run for an office. Taylor received the Whig nomination for president in 1848.

plantation (plan-TAY-shun): A plantation is a large farm that grows crops such as tobacco, sugarcane, or cotton. Zachary Taylor was a plantation owner and a slaveholder.

political parties (puh-LIT-uh-kul PAR-teez): Political parties are groups of people who share similar ideas about how to run a government. Members of the Whig political party opposed the Democratic Party.

politics (PAWL-uh-tiks): Politics refers to the actions and practices of the government. Taylor started his career in the military, not in politics.

preserve (pri-ZERV): If people preserve something, they keep it from harm or change. Taylor believed it was more important to preserve the Union than to extend slavery.

procession (pruh-SEH-shun): A procession is a group of people or vehicles moving along in a line. More than 100 carriages traveled in President Taylor's funeral procession.

promotion (pruh-MOH-shun): When people get a promotion, they advance in rank or importance. The US Army rewarded Taylor with promotions to higher ranks.

rallies (RAL-eez): Rallies are organized gatherings of people to show support for something or someone. In 1848, there were "Rough and Ready" political rallies for Zachary Taylor.

resolved (rih-ZAWLVD): If people resolved a problem, they found a successful solution to it. The slavery issue was not resolved during Taylor's presidency.

resources (REE-sor-suz): Resources are things that can be used to benefit people, such as oil or water. The government often controls land with valuable natural resources.

secretary of state (SEK-ruh-tayr-ee OF STAYT): The secretary of state is a close adviser to the president on relations with other countries. As secretary of state in 1808, James Madison recommended Taylor for military service.

territory (TAYR-uh-tor-ee): A territory is a land or region that belongs to a government. Northerners wanted to ban slavery in any territory won in the Mexican-American War.

treaties (TREE-teez): Treaties are formal agreements between nations. The United States and Britain agreed on the Clayton-Bulwer Treaty.

Union (YOON-yen): A union is the joining together of two or more people or groups of people, such as states. The Union is another name for the United States.

Whig Party (WIG PAR-tee): The Whig Party was a political party formed to oppose President Andrew Jackson. Taylor was a member of the Whig Party.

THE UNITED STATES GOVERNMENT

The United States government is divided into three equal branches: the executive, the legislative, and the judicial. This division helps prevent abuses of power because each branch has to answer to the other two. No one branch can become too powerful.

EXECUTIVE BRANCH

President
Vice President
Departments

The job of the executive branch is to enforce the laws. It is headed by the president, who serves as the spokesperson for the United States around the world. The president has the power to sign bills into law. He or she also appoints important officials, such as federal judges, who are then confirmed by the US Senate. The president is also the commander in chief of the US military. He or she is assisted by the vice president, who takes over if the president dies or cannot carry out the duties of the office.

The executive branch also includes various departments, each focused on a specific topic. They include the Defense Department, the Justice Department, and the Agriculture Department. The department heads, along with other officials such as the vice president, serve as the president's closest advisers, called the cabinet.

LEGISLATIVE BRANCH

Congress: Senate and the
House of Representatives

The job of the legislative branch is to make the laws. It consists of Congress, which is divided into two parts: the Senate and the House of Representatives. The Senate has 100 members, and the House of Representatives has 435 members. Each state has two senators. The number of representatives a state has varies depending on the state's population.

Besides making laws, Congress also passes budgets and enacts taxes. In addition, it is responsible for declaring war, maintaining the military, and regulating trade with other countries.

JUDICIAL BRANCH

Supreme Court
Courts of Appeals
District Courts

The job of the judicial branch is to interpret the laws. It consists of the nation's federal courts. Trials are held in district courts. During trials, judges must decide what laws mean and how they apply. Courts of appeals review the decisions made in district courts.

The nation's highest court is the Supreme Court. If someone disagrees with a court of appeals ruling, he or she can ask the Supreme Court to review it. The Supreme Court may refuse. The Supreme Court makes sure that decisions and laws do not violate the Constitution.

CHOOSING THE PRESIDENT

It may seem odd, but American voters don't elect the president directly. Instead, the president is chosen using what is called the Electoral College.

Each state gets as many votes in the Electoral College as its combined total of senators and representatives in Congress. For example, Iowa has two senators and four representatives, so it gets six electoral votes. Although the District of Columbia does not have any voting members in Congress, it gets three electoral votes. Usually, the candidate who wins the most votes in any given state receives all of that state's electoral votes.

To become president, a candidate must get more than half of the Electoral College votes. There are a total of 538 votes in the Electoral College, so a candidate needs 270 votes to win. If nobody receives 270 Electoral College votes, the House of Representatives chooses the president.

With the Electoral College system, the person who receives the most votes nationwide does not always receive the most electoral votes. This happened most recently in 2016, when Hillary Clinton received nearly 2.9 million more national votes than Donald J. Trump. Trump became president because he had more Electoral College votes.

The White House is the official home of the president of the United States. It is located at 1600 Pennsylvania Avenue NW in Washington, DC. In 1792, a contest was held to select the architect who would design the president's home. James Hoban won. Construction took eight years.

The first president, George Washington, never lived in the White House. The second president, John Adams, moved into the house in 1800, though the inside was not yet complete. During the War of 1812, British soldiers burned down much of the White House. It was rebuilt several years later.

The White House was changed through the years. Porches were added, and President Theodore Roosevelt added the West Wing. President William Taft changed the shape of the presidential office, making it into the famous Oval Office. While Harry Truman was president, the old house was discovered to be structurally weak. All the walls were reinforced with steel, and the rooms were rebuilt.

Today, the White House has 132 rooms (including 35 bathrooms), 28 fireplaces, and 3 elevators. It takes 570 gallons of paint to cover the outside of the six-story building. The White House provides the president with many ways to relax. It includes a putting green, a jogging track, a swimming pool, a basketball and tennis court, and beautifully landscaped gardens. The White House also has a movie theater, a billiard room, and a one-lane bowling alley.

PRESIDENTIAL PERKS

The job of president of the United States is challenging. It is probably one of the most stressful jobs in the world. Because of this, presidents are paid well, though not nearly as well as the leaders of large corporations. In 2020, the president earned $400,000 a year. Presidents also receive extra benefits that make the demanding job a little more appealing.

★ **Camp David:** In the 1940s, President Franklin D. Roosevelt chose this heavily wooded spot in the mountains of Maryland to be the presidential retreat, where presidents can relax. Even though it is a retreat, world business is conducted there. Most famously, President Jimmy Carter met with Middle Eastern leaders at Camp David in 1978. The result was a peace agreement between Israel and Egypt.

★ *Air Force One:* The president flies on a jet called *Air Force One*. It is a Boeing 747-200B that has been modified to meet the president's needs. *Air Force One* is the size of a large home. It is equipped with a dining room, sleeping quarters, a conference room, and office space. It also has two kitchens that can provide food for up to 100 people.

★ **The Secret Service:** While not the most glamorous of the president's perks, the Secret Service is one of the most important. The Secret Service is a group of highly trained agents who protect the president and the president's family.

★ **The Presidential State Car:** The presidential state car is a customized Cadillac limousine. It has been armored to protect the president in case of attack. Inside the plush car are a foldaway desk, an entertainment center, and a communications console.

★ **The Food:** The White House has five chefs who will make any food the president wants. The White House also has an extensive wine collection and vegetable and fruit gardens.

★ **Retirement:** A former president receives a pension, or retirement pay, of just under $208,000 a year. Former presidents also receive health care coverage and Secret Service protection for the rest of their lives.

QUALIFICATIONS

To run for president, a candidate must
- ★ be at least 35 years old
- ★ be a citizen who was born in the United States
- ★ have lived in the United States for 14 years

TERM OF OFFICE

A president's term of office is four years. No president can stay in office for more than two terms.

ELECTION DATE

The presidential election takes place every four years on the first Tuesday after November 1.

INAUGURATION DATE

Presidents are inaugurated on January 20.

OATH OF OFFICE

I do solemnly swear I will faithfully execute the office of the President of the United States and will to the best of my ability preserve, protect, and defend the Constitution of the United States.

WRITE A LETTER TO THE PRESIDENT

One of the best things about being a US citizen is that Americans get to participate in their government. They can speak out if they feel government leaders aren't doing their jobs. They can also praise leaders who are going the extra mile. Do you have something you'd like the president to do? Should the president worry more about the environment and the effects of climate change? Should the government spend more money on our schools? You can write a letter to the president to say how you feel!

> 1600 Pennsylvania Avenue NW
> Washington, DC 20500

You can even write a message to the president at **whitehouse.gov/contact**.

FOR MORE INFORMATION

BOOKS

Bausum, Ann. *Our Country's Presidents: A Complete Encyclopedia of the US Presidency.* Washington, DC: National Geographic, 2017.

Dunbar-Ortiz, Roxanne. *An Indigenous Peoples' History of the United States for Young People.* Boston, MA: Beacon Press, 2019.

Morlock, Jeremy P. *Abolitionists and Slave Owners.* New York, NY: PowerKids, 2019.

Rauf, Don. *The Mexican–American War.* New York, NY: Cavendish Square, 2018.

Roxburgh, Ellis. *The Seminole Wars.* New York, NY: Gareth Stevens, 2017.

INTERNET SITES

Visit our website for lots of links about
Zachary Taylor and other US presidents:

childsworld.com/links

Note to Parents, Teachers, and Librarians: We routinely verify our web links to make sure they are safe, active sites. Encourage your readers to check them out!